Landscapes
of Ireland

CLB 2778
© 1991 Colour Library Books Ltd., Godalming, Surrey, England
distributed by Outlet Book Company, Inc., a Random House Company,
225 Park Avenue South, New York, NY 10003.
Printed and bound in Hong Kong
ISBN 0- 517- 06043- 4
8 7 6 5 4 3 2 1

Landscapes of Ireland

CRESCENT BOOKS
NEW YORK

The Dromberg stone circle, near Glandore, County Cork.

The natural beauty for which Ireland is famed far and wide did not come about suddenly; it was the result of millions of years of slow development. Geologically, the island is one of the oldest areas of Western Europe. The granite of the Mountains of Mourne, which sweep down to the sea in County Down, formed 400 million years ago; only in the extreme northeast are the rocks much younger than 300 million years. But despite the immense age of the underlying rocks, it was only a few thousand years ago that the Ireland of today began to emerge.

Throughout the past three million years Ireland has been repeatedly overrun by vast sheets of ice which reached depths of thousands of metres. How many times the island was caught in the icy grip of the glaciers remains obscure, but the effects of the ice ages are undoubted, the millions of tons of ice slowly ground across the land having a profound effect on it. The rock was crushed beneath the moving ice, valleys gouged out and whole hills obliterated. For thousands of years the immense forces of geology slowly worked away in Ireland while life was banished from the whole region.

When the ice finally retreated northwards some ten thousand years ago it left behind a bare land, but a land with great promise. The pulverised rock left by the glaciers lay thirty metres thick across the lowlands. Known as boulder clay, this is one of nature's most fertile soils and has long been the basis for the verdancy of Ireland. In places, the vagaries of the moving ice deposited the boulder clay in drumlins – low, tear-shaped hills about a kilometre long. Between these hills and in depressions cut by the ice, water has since collected, forming the loughs and bogs characteristic of much of the island. The harder rocks of the west and south have no covering of rich glacial till, but they are still results of the rivers of ice. The limestone and sandstone of the south and the granite of Galway, Donegal and Mayo were carved and scraped by the glaciers into the shapes we see today. Though the land and rocks were sculpted by the end of the Ice

Ages, the same cannot be said of the landscape. For centuries after the solid ice retreated the snow mained, though it lay thinner and came less frequently with each passing year. The whole land was covered by tundra, the environment which still exists north of the arctic treeline and in high mountains. The treeless plains were covered with lichens, mosses and shrubs and roamed by one of the world's most remarkable deer.

The Irish elk was unknown until massive antlers were found in peat bogs. At first nobody knew where they had come from and numerous theories arose. It was only later that complete skeletons were found and the problem solved. It emerged that the Irish elk, or Megaloceros, was a genus of elk, about the size of a modern moose, which had antlers out of all proportion to its body. The two-metre-tall beast had antlers which spanned four metres from tip to tip. As the climate changed and man invaded the island, Megaloceros was pushed to extinction along with several other mammals.

The melting glaciers released millions upon millions of litres of water into the seas of the world and consequently raised the sea level. The Irish Sea was formed at this time, which had a permanent effect on the wildlife of Ireland. Reptiles love warm climates, indeed as cold-blooded animals they cannot survive in cold countries. When the Irish Sea cut Ireland off from Britain the climate was still distinctly chilly, so few reptiles could reach the island. The result is that only the common lizard became established and, as the land warmed, snakes were kept out by the waters of the Irish Sea.

Most of the Irish, however, know that the snakes did in fact reach Ireland. Indeed, it is said that they almost reached epidemic proportions at one time. But that was before Saint Patrick came to Ireland. When he was just sixteen, Patrick was torn from his civilised home in Roman Britain by Irish pirates and sold into slavery. After escaping back to Britain, Patrick returned to convert the Irish to Christianity. By all accounts he was highly successful and paganism took a downturn. Not only did he convert the people, he also banished the snakes by driving them all into the sea. Though none of the snakes of Britain is particularly deadly, Saint Patrick has been blessed for this action as much as for any other.

By the time Saint Patrick arrived in Ireland the perpetual ice had given way to a climate much the same as that enjoyed by the island today. Ireland is known as the Emerald Isle with good reason: it is one of the greenest lands in the world. Such verdancy is largely due to the climate which prevails across the island.

Ireland lies at the far western edge of the great Eurasian landmass and at the junction of the polar and tropical air masses. Its position on the edge of the Atlantic Ocean has a profound effect on the climate, especially as it is in the path of the warm Gulf Stream. The predominantly westerly winds pass across hundreds of kilometres of open water before they reach the island and are therefore heavy with moisture. The warm Gulf Stream, meanwhile, has a moderating effect on the air temperatures, giving warm winters and cool summers; a combination typical of maritime lands. It also adds more moisture to the air, making it even more prone to give rain. But warm, wet air in itself does not produce rain, it has to be cooled before it will release its moisture.

The boundary between cold polar air and warm tropical air is the precipitating factor in this process. Great swirls of air some 800 kilometres in diameter regularly cross the country. These depressions, as they are known, are areas of low air pressure characterised by fronts, which may be either warm or cold. A warm front occurs when cold air is followed by a belt of warm. The warm, moisture-laden winds rise slowly over the cold air and give steady, prolonged rain. Cold fronts occur when colder air undercuts warm air masses forcing them to rise and cool rapidly. This results in short, torrential downpours, not unlike those in the tropics. Both types of rain are extremely common in Ireland and, together with the mild maritime temperatures, are crucial contributory factors in creating the vital climatic conditions for the vegetation of this small, green island.

This modern climate did not arrive as soon as the glaciers retreated, nor did the vegetation associated with it. As the temperatures rose the tundra retreated before the advancing trees and shrubs. The birch and the hazel were the first to cover the land, for they are the hardiest of trees, but they were soon replaced by extensive stands of pine. Seven thousand years ago,

by which time Ireland was separated from Britain, the pine forests had been largely replaced by the beautiful deciduous stands which are still such a feature of Ireland. In many other countries as far north as Ireland the forests have not progressed beyond the pine stage. It is the warm Gulf Stream and the heavy rainfall which have made Ireland a land of broad-leaved trees.

Even so, some relics of the earlier forests remain. Hardy trees are scattered throughout the island and on the Burren, in County Clare, areas of hazel scrub can still be found. This area of high land faces the ocean south of Galway Bay and is exposed to the full rigours of the Atlantic storms. The limestone which forms these hills was scraped clean of soil during the Ice Ages and there is little to provide sustenance for plants. In such adverse conditions the original hardy forest cover has survived, undisturbed by later arrivals.

Away from the storm-blasted hills, the forests of Ireland are dominated by trees such as the oak, sycamore, ash, aspen and wych elm. Together, these and some rarer species, provide one of the richest and most productive ecosystems in the island. The deciduous woodland can be divided into a series of layers, each of which has a distinctive character. The topmost layer is made up of the tree canopy with its branches and leaves. Beneath this spreads the shrub layer where bushes and young trees grow in the shade of mature timber. In deciduous woodland it is usual to find evergreen shrubs in this layer as they can take advantage of the sunlight in the winter when the canopy is bare. A particularly clear example is to be found near Killarney in County Kerry, where holly bushes proliferate beneath the oak trees. The ground layer of the forest is littered with leaves fallen from above, giving a steady supply of food to its plants and animals. It is here that the wild flowers grow, often in early spring so as to avoid the leafed canopy. The daffodils, foxgloves, woundwort, honeysuckle and dogrose to be seen here are among the most spectacular in Ireland.

Invertebrates are by far the most numerous animals in Irish forests, with a host of slugs, arthropods and insects; but it is the mammals and birds that attract the most attention. All across Ireland mammals are generally small and, due to the island's early isolation, there are surprisingly few species. Birds, however, with their ability to cross the sea, have ensured that Ireland's forests are particularly rich in avian life. Many birds, of course, are only found in Ireland for part of the year, spending either the summer or the winter in other countries. The wood pigeon is one of those which stays throughout the year, but the similar turtle dove only visits during the summer. Great spotted woodpeckers fill the forests with their drumming, but it is the birds with large eyes which fill the small mammals with dread. The long-eared owl glides through the night on silent wings, stalking its prey by starlight. During the day its place is taken by the sparrow hawk, whose eyes glint beside its sharp beak.

But by no means all of Ireland became forest after the retreat of the glaciers; vast areas became bog. In many places the ice scraped clean the bedrock and gouged out massive hollows which filled with water when the glaciers retreated. Due to the lack of fertile soil, these lakes and ponds were low in mineral and nutritional elements and inhospitable to most vegetation. One of the few genus of plants able to survive in such waters is the sphagnum moss. There are more than 300 species of sphagnum, ranging in colour from light green to dark red, but all are broadly similar in structure. The thirty-centimetre-tall moss forms large clumps which float on the surface of still water. It floats due to air trapped within the plant tissues, but at the same time the plant cells are waterlogged, being as much as ninety per cent water. Once the moss is established it has a profound effect on its surroundings, inhibiting the growth of any other plant. The growing mass of vegetation soaks up the water, taking it from other plants and stopping the formation of soil. The metabolic process of the sphagnum moss exudes acid which can bring the pH value of the water down to less than five, a measure of acidity beyond the tolerance of most plants.

In the prehistoric lakes of Ireland the floating mats of sphagnum spread until they covered the entire surface and choked the water channels. As the moss grew the lower stems died off, but due to the air trapped within them they continued to float, though the increasing weight of the fresh growth pushed it beneath the water surface. The dense mass blocked the passage of air downwards so that there was no oxygen amongst the dead material. Together with the lack of minerals and the high acidity, the lack of oxygen prevented the rotting process which would normally have broken down the plants. Over the millennia the mats of floating moss have become denser and thicker until today they fill the entire lake basins. The fact that the moss sponge is now higher than the original water surface has not diminished the growth of the plant. Its spongy nature keeps enough stagnant water within reach for the plants to grow. In some instances the surface of the bog has managed to raise itself substantially above the surrounding land.

In other parts of Ireland, where there is particularly heavy rainfall, sphagnum has been able to gain a foothold wherever the drainage is poor, even on hillsides. Once established, the moss follows a similar pattern, developing a thick mass of water-laden matter. In such cases the mat is only loosely linked to the hill and is remarkably unstable. On occasion an apparently solid hillside will suddenly writhe, shift and slide into the valley below; one of the more unnerving sights in Ireland.

The bogs of Ireland, with their stagnant water, low mineral content and high acidity, are a peculiar habitat which makes great demands upon its inhabitants. Apart from the bog moss there are scattered stands of black bog rush and the colourful bog asphodel, while the straggling cranberry is common in wetter bogs. Another, more sinister, plant that is found on Irish bogs has the attractive name of sundew. The sundew needs far more minerals than the bog can provide, so it traps and digests insects. The bright red traps are covered with stalks topped by a drop of liquid. This liquid attracts insects, but it is in reality a sticky substance which entangles them. The stalks will then exude an enzyme which digests the insect, allowing the plant to absorb minerals from its prey. Luckily for the abundant insect life of the bogs, the exotic sundew is not one of the commonest plants to be found in Ireland.

Not all the lakes which formed after the Ice Ages filled with sphagnum. On extensive bodies of water a strong, steady wind is able to produce substantial waves which break up the mats of moss. In Ireland some of these stretches of water are so wide and treacherous that they are referred to as inland seas. The yachtsmen and anglers of the loughs have to take similar precautions to those taken when putting to sea, if they are to avoid tragedy. The largest of these 'seas' is Lough Neagh, which straddles the borders of Counties Antrim, Down, Armagh, Tyrone and Derry. This 388-square-kilometre stretch of water is set in broad, flat countryside and so lacks the scenic grandeur of other loughs which lie in the mountains. The low relief around the lough is reflected beneath the waters, rather than on them, for the lakebed is only twelve metres below the surface.

Bog water may stand stagnant for years, but eventually it will leave the moss and sparkle through the streams and into the flowing rivers. The rivers and loughs of Ireland are famous the world over for their clarity, beauty and wildlife. As with the bogs, mountains and forests, the rivers clearly show the results of glaciation. Where the ice left the mountains the streams leap down steep slopes in glittering splashes, but the lowlands are characterised by gentle, stately flows, all of them rich in wildlife. The streams of the hills and mountains are necessarily fast-flowing as they tumble down the slopes and falls. In such conditions there are few plants, but the detritus from the surrounding land is enough to provide food for insect larvae and so for trout. It is where the streams become slightly slower that the wildlife is most abundant. Plants grow in the silty bottom and amongst the gravels of the riverbed, and these provide cover and food for a whole host of animals. There are molluscs, hydra and flatworms amongst the smaller animals, though it is the larger creatures, such as fish and birds, which form such an essential part of the river scene.

Many species of insect go through a larval stage in the rivers of Ireland, and the adults are naturally most often seen nearby. Dragonflies are probably the most spectacular of these insects, darting across the water on their iridescent wings. Fish dominate the fauna beneath the surface, eating as they do a wide variety of plant and animal matter. Salmon come up the waters of Ireland to spawn, while trout may likewise migrate or remain, depending on the species. Dozens of other fish inhabit the rivers and loughs, but one is peculiarly Irish. The twaite shad is an ocean fish which feeds in estuaries, but in the lakes of Killarney in County Kerry a small population was once cut off from the sea. Interestingly it has now developed into a distinctly separate form of the same fish.

Irish rivers, unlike those of many other countries, have not shaped the land to suit themselves. Instead, the landscape has determined the course and shape of the rivers, from their sources to the sea. Those that rise on the seaward slopes of the mountains tumble down the rocks directly into the surf and never have a chance to develop a wide-ranging fauna. Other rivers move inland from the mountains across the central plain of Ireland, most of them eventually reaching the Shannon.

The Shannon below Limerick is unusual amongst Irish rivers in having a long, wide estuary. Like all the features of the Irish coast, the Shannon Estuary is the result of long geological processes. The west coast has been pounded for centuries by the powerful waves of Atlantic storms and broken into a series of peninsulas, bays and islands. In prehistoric times, according to legend, one of the islands was inhabited by the Fomorians, who could control the fog and storms of the ocean and impose blight upon crops. Finally, the Irish had had enough of the Fomorians and, after a violent battle, drove them into the sea.

The surf-pounded coast of the west is at its most spectacular in the south, where the towering peninsulas of Dingle, Beara and Kenmare reach out into the ocean. The long bays between the peninsulas are, in fact, ancient river valleys which were drowned when the sea level rose after the Ice Ages. But even the romantic, surf-sprayed shores of the southwest dwindle by comparison to the Cliffs of Moher in County Clare. These 200-metre-tall cliffs rise sheer from the crashing waves below and are circled by screaming sea birds. North of the cliffs lies Galway Bay, where scenic beauty reaches its highest expression.

Of all the coastal features of Ireland the most enigmatic is to be found in County Antrim. Legend has it that in the third century Finn MacCool was the leader of a band of warrior-poets known as the Fianna Eireann. In an effort to get at his rival giant Finn Gall in Scotland, MacCool began to build a causeway across the North Channel. He never finished and only the massive piles remain to form the Giant's Causeway, north of Bushmills. Modern scientists, however, maintain that the polygonal columns were created when large amounts of lava erupted from the earth and gradually cooled.

The east coast of Ireland has escaped the fearful battering of the waves received by the west and is made of less resistant rocks. This is a seaboard characterised by sweeping, golden sands and smooth contours, which are far more inviting to seafarers than the rugged west.

It was upon that shore that eager eyes gazed some 8,000 years ago. Britain had long been inhabited by people who hunted and fished and gathered plants for food. By 6,000 BC these people had developed a type of boat in which they could put to sea and be reasonably sure that they would survive. The surprisingly sturdy craft were built around a basic wooden frame with rib-like bracing struts, the whole construction being made watertight by a covering of skins. The fishermen who sailed off the western coasts of Pembroke, Galloway and Kintyre must have often caught sight of a strange land on the horizon. Eventually, some of them had the courage to land and even settle on the mysterious shores. The first people had come to Ireland. They found a beautiful but wild work of nature and began to tame it. Ever since that moment man has had a profound effect on Ireland and its landscapes.

The Mesolithic, or middle stone age, to which these first Irish people belonged, was characterised by specialised hunting and gathering. Fishing communities were typical of the times and the remains of several have been found along the coasts and rivers of Ireland. One of the oldest of these was discovered in Toome Bay, on Lough Neagh in County Antrim. Settlements of such people are usually identified by the vast rubbish tips, known as middens, of shells and fishbones which can still be seen today.

Village dumps are neither particularly useful nor aesthetic legacies, but the first Irish bequeathed another invention to later generations: their boats. For millennia the Irish have put to sea in the skin-covered wooden craft of the Mesolithic fishermen. Today they are known as currachs and are mainly used by the men of Aran, who put to sea in search of fish much as their ancestors did thousands of years ago.

A more enterprising exponent of the currach was a medieval monk whose exploits are recounted in many tales. Saint Brendan was born in Tralee in AD 484 and became a monk early in life, quickly rising to a position of prominence. At this time communications with ecclesiastical centres outside Ireland had been broken by the fall of the Roman Empire. Brendan set out to re-establish such links. He put to sea in a large currach and headed for the Hebrides, where he met Saint Columba. Saint Brendan later reached mainland Scotland, Wales and Brittany in the course of his work. According to the early Irish epic *Voyage of Brendan*, the sailor monk later went on to discover new lands to the west of Ireland. Since medieval scholars knew that the world ended in the grey Atlantic, such adventures were written off as fables.

More recent investigations of the tales, however, reveal many similarities between Saint Brendan's discoveries and real lands. The Canary Islands, the Faeroes, the Azores, Madeira, Iceland, Newfoundland, the West Indies and Florida have all been claimed as landfalls of Saint Brendan. In an effort to prove that Saint Brendan could have achieved all this, three men set sail in 1977 from Ireland in a currach. Over five thousand kilometres later the small craft arrived in Newfoundland, proving a point which had been hotly debated. Most scholars agree that the *Voyage of Brendan* is a collection of tales which Irish sailors had brought home, though how accurate the modern interpretations are remains open to question.

Similar craft brought the Neolithic settlers to Ireland some centuries after the Mesolithic Irish. The new people brought with them staggering advances in culture, technology and lifestyle. They were farmers and pastoralists, growing grain and herding cattle. They came to Ireland and were confronted by the land of forest and bog which nature had shaped. With the level of technology available to the Neolithic farmers the exploitation of the land was at once dramatic and transitory.

The farmers moved in small groups of perhaps a few families, which led a semi-settled way of life. When they found a suitable tract of forest, the farmers would hack down the trees and burn off the undergrowth. That done, a village be built from the felled timber, and grain would be sown on the cleared land. Working without the benefit of the plough or an understanding of fertilisers, the early farmers could not properly exploit the soil. Within a few years, the yield of the patch of cleared land would fall. The farming group would then move on to clear and burn another patch of forest.

Given this destructive activity on the part of numerous groups of early farmers, it might be thought that Ireland's forests would have been destroyed within a few years. But the soil of Ireland is surprisingly fertile and the natural vegetation highly resilient. Seeds of the woodland plants remained in the soil throughout the few years of cultivation and sprang to life as soon as they had a chance. Within a few seasons the shrubs would dominate the land, interspersed with saplings. Within a few seasons, the cleared area would have reverted to forest as the natural order reasserted itself.

A more permanent effect on the landscape came with improvements in agriculture which allowed communities to settle and found villages. Prosperity increased and the people were able to turn their minds to things other than mere survival. Tools and weapons became much more efficient, beautiful and decorative, far removed from the crude style of the slash and burn era. The huts in which these people lived were better constructions than had been the case earlier and their villages were thoughtfully designed and laid out.

The landscape of the country was beginning to change. For the first time in the immensely long story of Ireland, which dates back 400 million years, an influence other than that of nature began to take a hand. Most noticeable was the fact that forests no longer reasserted themselves after a few years, for the men did not move on to new areas. Instead, forests were cleared for good. Many of the tracts of woodland felled by those remote ancestors of the Irish have never supported a tree since. They have been continually cultivated.

This absence of trees which now reaches across much of the country is taken almost for granted by the Irish of today. It is not recognised as the legacy of early man. More obviously the marks of man are the numerous material remains which have survived the centuries. On a gorse-covered slope above Doagh, County Antrim, stands a tall, weathered stone which is pierced by a time-worn hole. This is just one of the many megalithic monuments which can be found across Ireland. Megalith means quite simply 'large stone', but the term refers to prehistoric monuments where the construction features massive rocks. Quite how old the Doagh Stone is nobody is quite sure, but its purpose can be guessed at. Even today it is known that betrothed couples should clasp hands through the hole. It would seem that the solitary stone performed some sort of role in a fertility cult.

Such megaliths do not always stand alone in Ireland. The Proleek Dolmen, near Ballymascanlan in County Louth, is a group of four stones. Three of the stones stand upright and support the fourth a metre or so above the ground. As with the Doagh Stone, a local belief may point to its original function. It is considered lucky to throw a pebble at the stones, but only if it remains perched on the capstone. A far more extensive complex of stones is to be found eighty kilometres to the northwest at Beaghmore, near Cookstown.

The great complex of stone circles, cairns and alignments at Beaghmore was found entirely by accident just three decades ago. When peat cutters began to work the area they frequently came across boulders beneath the surface which should not have been there. It was only when several stones had been uncovered that their regular layout was revealed and archaeologists called in. The peat has only been cleared from part of the site, but already an extensive layout has emerge. There are three pairs of circles, each many metres in diameter and containing dozens of megaliths. One of the circles, which stands on its own, is filled with hundreds of small, upright stones. The circles are connected to straight lines of uprights which diverge at tangents. Obviously this was a major centre for prehistoric man, though its purpose can only be guessed. It is one of many circles and complexes which are to be found right across Ireland and which form an important part of the landscape.

The proliferation of megalithic monuments seems to have been associated with the arrival in Ireland of a fresh group of invaders: the Beaker People. Exactly where this new people came from remains obscure, but an Iberian origin seems most likely. These enigmatic people gained their name from the distinctive beaker-style pots with which they insisted on being buried. It is uncertain if the coming of the Beaker Culture represents the movement of a whole nation or of only a few individuals. People like to be buried with items they value, and the Beaker men were interred with decidedly warlike grave goods. This may point towards a warrior society, indicating a violent invasion which perhaps established a military aristocracy.

Whatever the nature of the Beaker takeover, their culture and way of life soon dominated Ireland. They were expert workers of copper and bronze – materials previously unknown in Ireland. Ireland was not, however, deficient in the raw materials for metallurgy. In fact the island was so rich in readily accessible ores that it became a bastion of the culture. It may have been these deposits which first attracted the Beaker people to Europe's westernmost island. The fame of Irish goods at this time reached right across Europe, even as far as Greece, where they have turned up during excavations at Mycenae.

The people of Megalithic times buried their dead with great care and, it can be assumed, elaborate ritual. Chambers and passages were constructed of massive blocks of stone and then covered with mounds of stones and earth. Such tombs proliferate throughout Ireland, but the largest and best known are at Brugh Na Boinne in County Meath.

Newgrange, the largest of the three tombs, dates back to about 3,100 BC when the building of such tombs was at its height and hundreds of them were scattered across Ireland. It is a truly remarkable achievement of a people who are often considered to have been primitive and uncivilised. The mound which covers the burial chambers is ninety metres in diameter and originally stood to a height of fifteen metres. Though it contains nearly 200,000 tons of stone and rock, the builders were not content with sheer size. The carefully constructed alternate layers of turves and stones were remarkably stable, while channels direct water away from the burial chambers. The whole mound was given a final covering of glittering quartz pebbles, and kept in place by a ring of kerb-stones.

The greatest finery, however, was reserved for the entrance. The kerb-stones were topped by a three-metre-tall wall of quartz for some thirty metres to either side. Lying in front of the entrance is a megalith some three metres long and over a metre high. On the surface of the rock are carved numerous swirls, spirals and geometric designs. Above the entrance, which would originally have been closed, is a unique feature: a stone hides a small box from which a slit opens into the interior of the mound.

Within the mound is the tomb itself. A twenty-metre-long passage runs into the heart of the mound. The walls of the tunnel are constructed of megaliths up to one-and-a-half-metres tall and are decorated with numerous carvings and designs. The passage leads to a fine central chamber with a corbelled dome roof which reaches a height of six metres. This also boasts decorated stone carvings. Off this central chamber open three smaller chambers, which presumably held the bodies of the dead.

The massive stones were laid with a precision typical of the time. In the furthest chamber this exactness is revealed in startling fashion. Before dawn on midwinter morning, when the outer entrance is closed, the inner tomb is silent and black. But as the sun rises above the horizon its pale rays bathe the mound in light. At that precise moment a ray of light flashes through the box slit and streaks the entire length of the passage to splash over the rear wall of the furthest chamber, bathing the dark recesses with an unearthly glow. Why the ancient Irish needed to flood their dead with light once a year, we do not know, but the engineering involved reveals the builders to have been skilled and competent. A thousand years ago Newgrange and other nearby burial mounds were broken into by the Vikings and pillaged of their contents.

Scattered throughout Ireland are hundreds of megalithic burial mounds, though few are as spectacular as those at Brugh Na Boinne. That at Labbacallee in County Cork incorporates several exceptionally large megaliths, including one roof-slab which measures eight metres by five metres. In the northern part of the island a distinctive form of tomb developed known as the court cairn design, the most extensive example of which is to be found at Creevykeel, County Sligo.

Long after the megalith builders had disappeared from the stage of history, their tombs were taken over by another, more secretive, people. Late at night groups of beautiful, fair-haired people were seen creeping from hidden doors within the mounds and gentle music heard lilting on the breeze. If they thought anyone was watching them, however, the dancers would quickly flit back to their home beneath the ground. Sometimes they would invite someone whom they had met down into the ground with them. There he would find an incredibly beautiful place where he feasted on exquisite food in marble halls. But guests in this wonderful world had to be careful, for a full year passed for every half hour spent in fairyland.

As the Bronze Age burial mounds fell out of use a new metal, iron, arrived in Ireland and with it a new people who have dominated the land ever since: the Celts. This remarkable people originated around the Rhine, but before the seventh century BC they had begun to spread. The Celts gloried in fighting, not only with their neighbours but also with each other. Their ferocity brought them conquests as far afield as Asia Minor and Spain and in 390 BC they even captured and pillaged Rome. The vast territories taken over by the Celts was never welded into a unified state, however, for the tribes were fiercely independent and never stopped fighting each other.

When the Celts came to Ireland around the fifth century BC they introduced their society of tribal kings, ruled by overkings who in turn were governed by a high king. In practice the system never worked and Ireland was reduced to a collection of warring tribes who stuck to their loyalties only when it suited them. To protect themselves from the roaming bands of warriors the Celts built tribal strongholds. These magnificent centres have long been deserted, but the massive ramparts remain an important feature of the Irish landscape.

The most dramatically sited of all these Iron Age fortresses is surely Dun Aengus on Inishmore, the largest of the Aran Islands. It is perched atop a sheer cliff which drops sixty metres to the pounding Atlantic surf. Standing with its back to this cliff, the semi-circular fortress takes the best possible advantage of its windswept position. The concentric walls are a superb defence, with the outer construction embracing four hectares and the inner wall standing six metres tall and just over five metres thick. Between the outer and second walls is a collection of standing stones. Unlike the megaliths of an earlier age, these stones had no religious significance: they were a purely defensive measure designed to disrupt any attacking formation and make passage impossible for chariots, a favourite war-machine of the Celts.

Far from the Aran Islands stands a far more important, if less well sited, fortress. Two thousand years ago the Ui Néill kings ruled all of northern Ireland from the Hill of Tara. The low hill contains a remarkable collection of structures within just a thousand metres. Tara has had importance for the Irish for more than four thousand years, through all the changes of culture and government.

The earliest structure at Tara is the Mound of the Hostages, a passage grave much like Newgrange, which has been dated to around 2,100 BC. Unlike its larger counterpart, the Mound of the Hostages is a simple, clay-covered mound without elaborate ornamentation. Even so, when archaeologists excavated the tomb, work which began in 1955 and was completed in 1959, it was found to contain a magnificent collection of artefacts. The mound continued to be used for burials for nearly a millennium, an indication of its importance. The tomb was later included in the Royal Enclosure, which dates from the Iron Age. This mighty earthwork is over 300 metres across and was originally strengthened by a wooden palisade. Within the enclosure are two smaller, but more formidable, defences. The smaller earthworks are surrounded by two lines of banks and ditches and were, perhaps, the citadel of the defences.

On a mound within the larger of the inner earthworks stands the Lia Fail. Originally this highly significant block of stone stood near to the Mound of the Hostages, which may point to megalithic origins. Whatever its original function, the stone was put to good use by the kings of Tara. At the coronation ceremony the stone was said to roar its approval if the rightful king was being crowned. The Lia Fail is not the only inauguration stone to be found in Ireland. Near Londonderry stands Saint Columb's Stone which was used for the recognition of chiefs of the O'Dohertys. In the top of the two-metre-square stone are two foot-sized depressions in which the chief would stand. Another great stone was taken from Ireland by the Scots, who were originally Irish, when they migrated across the sea to Argyll in the fifth century AD. The stone became the inauguration symbol of the Kingdom of Dalriada, and later of Scotland. In 1296 King Edward I of England took the stone to Westminster and it is now set in the coronation throne of the monarchs of Great Britain.

Superstitious awe of such stones was not always popular with the early Christian missionaries, and Tara saw a dramatic confrontation in AD 433. The pagan King of Tara forbade Saint Patrick from lighting a paschal fire at Easter. Saint Patrick promptly lit a fire within sight of the Lia Fail, thus enhancing the importance of Christianity in Ireland.

The spread of the new religion from Romanised Britain had a profound effect on Ireland, both spiritually and physically. Saint Patrick was not, despite what every Irishman says, the first Christian missionary to Ireland. Palladius came to Ireland in AD 431 on the instructions of the Bishop of Auxerre; but he was not concerned with evangelism, only with preaching to the converted. Saint Patrick's great achievement was the establishment of a movement. He inspired a group of Christians who rapidly spread across Ireland and set out a programme which assured rapid conversion.

The missionaries did not attempt to destroy local traditions, they preferred to mould and adapt them to Christian ideals. Likewise, they did not openly attack the influential Druids and as a result were not themselves threatened; not a single martyrdom was recorded. Within a few decades almost the whole island was Christian and promptly went its own way. In a land virtually devoid of towns or unity, a diocesan organisation could not survive. The petty kingdoms and fragmented nature of Irish society inclined towards smaller units, and monasteries flourished, the individual monasteries being loosely linked under the auspices of a larger house. Before long, abbots were the leaders of Irish Christians and they adhered to traditional

or peculiarly Irish practices. The church as a whole drifted away from Roman teachings and became known as Celtic Christianity.

The impact of the new religion on the countryside was far-reaching in its effects. Sacred pagan glades and streams were replaced in importance by wooden and stone-built churches and monasteries. Across most of Ireland rectangular wooden churches proliferated after conversion. None of these has survived the intervening centuries, but descriptions of them abound. They were about five metres long, two metres wide and surmounted by steeply pitched roofs. Such unassuming structures soon became the centre of landscape as the lives of the people began to focus around them.

Though they have gone, the small wooden churches can still be seen in the stone churches which replaced them. Tradition is amazingly strong in Ireland and when stone replaced timber in the late eighth century, churches continued to be built in the same manner. On Saint Macdara's Island, off the Connemara coast, stands a small church which was built with stone ornamentation resembling heavy timber beams and shingles. Small churches of this type continued to be built for centuries until a very different style was introduced to Ireland from Europe in the twelfth century.

Even more conservative were the churches built in Western Ireland. There, the monks did not even take to the mock-timber construction. In part this is explained by the fact that there were never many trees in the West. The people had long been building in stone and the monks simply adapted the traditional corbel construction to their own purposes. On Skellig Michael, off the Kerry Coast, stands a beautiful example of such a monastery. Unfortunately, the traditional design persisted for so long that it is impossible to date the structure accurately. It was built sometime between the ninth and thirteenth centuries and that is all that can be said.

Perched 150 metres up on an isolated crag high above the ocean, the monastery is reached by a long flight of 670 ancient steps. The monks' cells and oratory were built of a dry-stone construction which has survived centuries of Atlantic storms. The roofs were formed by corbelling; the slight overlapping of each course of stones until a dome is created. The round buildings usually produced are immensely strong, if a little draughty. Monks seeking a holy life of abstemious conditions would have found such structures ideal. The dry-stone construction of these buildings can be traced right back to the Neolithic graves of Brugh Na Boinne. It is even possible that the houses of ancient man were round beehive huts of corbel design.

Like their eastern colleagues, the monks of the West felt compelled to build small, rectangular churches. The corbelled vault is at its strongest when used for domes, but when bridging long rectangular spaces it tends to sag. Over the centuries the majority of these structures have collapsed, the Gallarus Oratory on the Dingle Peninsula being one of the few exceptions.

A far more noticeable feature of ecclesiastical architecture in Ireland is the round tower which dominates so many views. The narrow towers are more like turrets rising up to thirty-six metres above the ground. Peculiarly Irish, these structures are associated with about 120 monasteries throughout the island, but their exact purpose remains a mystery. Perhaps they were belfries, as their height suggests, or even storehouses. The position of the door, however, indicates a more vital function. The only entrance is usually some four metres above ground level and can only be reached by a ladder. The towers date from the ninth to twelfth centuries, the days of the Viking attacks. It follows that they may have been built as secure refuges for the monks to hide in when the fierce Norsemen pillaged their monasteries.

Of the many round towers known to have been built, only about seventy remain standing, and those mostly in ruins; the fine, twenty-six-metre-tall tower on the Rock of Cashel being a notable exception. Also on the 150-metre-high rock is Cormac's Chapel, a fine example of the style which replaced mock-timber in church building. As the capital of the Kings of Munster it was only fit that Cashel should see the first of any new trend. Many years earlier the Rock had been the venue for one of Saint Patrick's most important sermons. It was here that he explained the concept of the Trinity by using a shamrock leaf and thereby converted the pagan king. The site was marked by the construction of the chapel in 1127 by the King of Munster and Bishop of Cashel, Cormac MacCarthy.

The Rock of Cashel ceased to be the capital of the MacCarthy Kings of Munster in 1101 when it was turned over to the church as a purely ecclesiastical site. In 1317 it re-entered history in a blood-drenched manner when Scottish troops marched through the area on their way to Nenagh. On June 24th, 1314, Robert the Bruce, King of Scotland, defeated Edward II of England on the banks of the Bannock Burn in southern Scotland. He was therefore free to pursue his dream of a united Celtic Kingdom. Consequently, as part of this plan, Edward Bruce, Robert's brother, landed at Larne in 1315 with a powerful force.

Unfortunately for Robert, Edward thought that pillaging and plundering his prospective kingdom would endear him to his subjects. It didn't and Edward was killed at Faught in 1318. In the meantime, his armies had raided through Ulster, Leinster and had reached as far into Munster as Cashel.

When not involved with such incursions the ordinary people of Ireland had been quietly getting on with their lives. The advances in church architecture had passed them by, except to remind them of the glory of God, but advances in agriculture had not. The farming of the ordinary Irishman had progressed far beyond the simple slash and burn techniques of his remote ancestors. Cattle had first been domesticated in Greece about 6,000 BC and pigs in Russia somewhat earlier, but neither had arrived in Ireland with the first settlers. The prospect of milk and meat from cattle and delicacies such as bacon and ham from fast-fattening pigs was a great attraction. The use of these domesticated animals spread rapidly across Europe, including Ireland, though whether by trade or war remains obscure.

More useful than other beasts for milk production since their yield was greater, the cow also provided meat. Perhaps more vital was the fact that oxen could be used to pull the ploughs which made possible greater grain production. Cereals, after all, were still the staple food of Ireland. Cattle were also of prime importance in the conduct of warfare between the country's various tiny kingdoms. Upon his accession a petty king or *ri* was expected to prove his fitness to rule by embarking on a cattle raid into his enemies' territories. The greatest cattle raid of all was the cattle raid of Cooley, which is recorded in *The Yellow Book of Lecan*. On this occasion Maeve, Queen of Connaught, led her entire army into Ulster to steal the brown bull of Cooley and was met by only one man. That man was Cu Chulainn, one of the most important heroes in Irish legend. For many days he killed the successive champions of Maeve and in this way he stopped the advance of the Connaught army long enough for the Ulster warriors to come to his aid. Though the cattle raid of Cooley is the subject of a great saga and contains much fanciful information, it is indicative both of the importance of cattle and of the part raiding played in early Irish society.

When they embarked on these raids into enemy territory, the Celts rarely went on foot. Then, as now, the Irish were great horse breeders and chariots were the favoured war machines. Horses had been known in Western Europe since before the Ice Ages, but for a long time all that man could think of doing with them was to kill and eat them. The idea of riding horses first occurred to man out on the Eurasian steppes about four thousand years ago, but only spread slowly across the rest of the world. By the time the Celts arrived in Ireland, however, the horse was well established as a beast of burden and a mode of transport.

The accomplishment of horse riding by the Irish was a great boon to the pookas. Pookas are black horses or donkeys with fiery red eyes, which roam the countryside at night. When they spy someone alone they will nuzzle up to him, almost asking to be ridden home. But once the hapless victim has mounted all signs of friendliness vanish. The powerful beast gallops off across the countryside on a terrifying ride, crashing through rivers, over hedges and between trees at breakneck speed. Finally, the pooka will throw its petrified and dishevelled rider into a muddy pond or thorny bush, leaving him to find his own way home. These days pookas are normally encountered only after the pubs have shut.

The introduction of pigs to the British Isles, and thence to Ireland, was such an important event that it found its way into legend. The *Red Book of Hergest* records an ancient Celtic tale which describes how pigs first come to Gwynedd. Gwydion, a native of Gwynedd, heard of some strange new animals which were gifts to Pryderi, Lord of Dyfed, from Arawn, King of Annwn. After Gwydion swindled Pryderi of his pigs, he fled to his own king, Math, son of Mathonwy, for protection. The humble swine was valued so highly in those days that Pryderi gathered together all his warriors and marched north where they met the army of Math. For days the fighting continued, with heavy casualties on either side. The bloodshed was only brought to an end when Gwydion slew Pryderi in single combat.

There is nothing that a healthy pig likes more than to munch acorns and root around for food in the undergrowth. Since the Celts were no more inclined to unnecessary work than anybody else, they simply set a swineherd to watch the pigs as they found their own food. The taste that these early Irish acquired for pork and bacon meant that thousands of pigs were bred to graze the forests. There they industriously ate vast quantities and, incidentally, destroyed great areas of forest. The seeds that the pigs ate did not have a chance to germinate and those that did start to grow were promptly eaten. Over the years no new trees grew to take the place of their predecessors and, when the old trees fell, much of the forest became open grass or scrubland.

Sheep were introduced onto any likely patch of grassland and continued the work of the pigs by trimming any vegetation so close that no sapling stood much chance of surviving its first year. Unlike the pigs, sheep were not kept for their meat. Their

wool was spun into yarn. This in turn provided the basis for the woven and knitted garments which kept the people warm. The brat, a shoulder-fastened cloak, was the chief garment of both men and women at the time. It was here that the Irish displayed their wealth. The finest wool which could be afforded was woven into the brat and the penannular brooches which fastened the cloak in place became the hallmark of fine Irish metalwork. The clearing of the forests which had been embarked upon by the slash and burn farmers and continued by the Bronze Age Irish was accelerated as a consequence of man's proclivity for meat and clothing.

As the forests disappeared, another great feature of Ireland's landscape began to be tapped by man. When man first came to Ireland, peat bogs covered nearly one seventh of the total land area and were a considerable nuisance. They were places devoid of agricultural or hunting potential, while the treacherous underfoot conditions made them places to avoid. Before long, however, it was realised that the half-rotted moss beneath the bog surface burnt surprisingly well. At first the gathering in of peat was a rather haphazard business. The cut turves take some time to dry sufficiently to be used and a settled life had to be established before the peat could be properly exploited. For many years turf fires were the principal form of heating in Irish homes and the peculiar odour of burning peat was a great feature of Irish life.

Peat bogs are amazingly wet places and the collection of peat for fires is a long process. In the early days of peat exploitation it was cut with long-hafted spades into rectangular blocks and laid on the surface of the bog to dry. When first dug, peat contains as much as ninety per cent water and takes some time to dry enough to become useful. The stacks of peat sods were a familiar sight across much of Ireland in prehistoric times and have remained so to the present day. More recently, a mechanized form of peat cutting has come into favour. A large dredger will gouge out quantities of peat. This is then chopped up and reconstituted into regular-sized blocks which are then laid out for drying. Millions of tons of peat are now consumed in Ireland every year and it is used to generate an important proportion of the country's electricity; a distant cry from the domestic turf fire of the Celts.

By the time the first Christian missionaries came to Ireland, agriculture had settled into a fairly steady pattern which was gradually shaping and moulding the landscape to suit itself. The native tradition had been changed by contact with the rather more advanced Roman system to the east. Not that the Irish took to building grand villas with underfloor heating. Instead, they continually raided the western coasts of Britain in search of gold and slaves. Inevitably, some of the slaves they brought back had previously been farmers, plodding their quiet way across the fields of Britain. The Irish naturally set their new acquisitions to work in the fields of Ireland, where they performed much more productively than had the native Irish.

Pigs were still herded in the remaining forests, as they had been for centuries, while cattle and sheep were put out to pasture. Around the villages of Ireland, for there were no towns or cities, the fields spread out in narrow strips. Cereals such as wheat, barley and oats were perhaps most important and Ireland was scattered with small villages surrounded by wide fields ripe with golden grain. Techniques of grain production were not up to the standards of today and a field of wheat did not only contain wheat. Weeds proliferated amongst the ears of grain and the golden fields were sprinkled with green. When the crop was harvested with the simple sickles and hooks of the time, the seeds of the weeds were gathered in as well. The commonest way of eating cereal was pottage, a mass of boiled flour, vegetables and anything else that was handy. The weeds went in as well and added to the flavour. In bad years the grain fields would have been more predominantly green and weeds would form an important part of the diet.

Before the Roman influence was felt, Irish communities rarely grew their own fruit and vegetables. The landscape was dominated by bogs, forests, sheep-grazed grassland and villages with their grain fields. Any fruit that was consumed would be gathered in the wild land that remained, and pretty much the same was true of vegetables. The small cottage surrounded by its patch of land on which are grown vegetables and fruit was unknown at the time, but a start was being made.

Nuts, wild fruit, scrawny carrots and nettles had been known in Ireland for many years and were usually eaten raw or stewed in a pottage. The gathering of such wild products was not entirely haphazard. Particularly fine blackberry patches and tree groves were undoubtedly highly prized and possibly the property of a village. The later Brehon Laws, which date to the eighth century, place definite values upon mature and immature nut and fruit trees with appropriate penalties for damaging them. These laws, which are also known as Feinechus, would reveal much about Irish society and agriculture, but unfortunately they are written in such an obscure form of Gaelic that any translation is at best an educated guess. The production of grain naturally led to the production of beer, and whiskey was not far behind. Indeed, the

Celts were known even in Classical times as prodigious drinkers: the average Irishman was well able to outlast a Roman when it came to alcohol. Beer gave an interesting byproduct in the form of vinegar, which was widely used as a condiment and, diluted, as a drink.

The Roman occupation of Britain, however, brought many new crop varieties within reach of Ireland. Roman apples and pears were much larger and sweeter than the crab apples which the Celts were used to eating and were probably carried across the Irish Sea fairly rapidly. The sweet cherry which the Romans also brought was probably much rarer in Ireland. The Irish consumption of vegetables also benefited from trade with and raids on Roman Britain. The eastern island produced richer and more substantial varieties of carrots and other root crops which were soon taken up by the Irish. Meanwhile, onions, radishes, lettuces and marrows were all being seen in Ireland for the first time, as was a wide variety of edible fungi not native to Ireland. Many of the less hardy plants, such as cucumbers and peaches, may have been grown in Ireland, but it is more likely that they were only known through trade. Either way, they disappeared from Ireland soon after the Roman withdrawal from Britain.

This great influx of new and improved vegetables and fruits introduced to Ireland the idea of a domestic garden separate from the shared grain field. The grazing of herd animals, pig breeding in sties, cereal production and the garden were to be the controlling influence on Ireland's landscape for a thousand years after the fall of Roman Britain. Ireland continued to develop along these lines until another foreign crop came to the island and changed the scenery forever.

High up in the Andes of South America the all-conquering Spaniards marched into the fabulous cities of the Incas and wrested from them their gold and their silver. The Conquistadors were dazzled by the stupendous wealth that they had seized. But among the solid gold tables and tons of silver they sent back to Spain was an odd collection of plants. At the same time Sir Walter Raleigh, who owned large amounts of land in Ireland, was a favourite of the English Queen Elizabeth and had numerous connections in the New World. Through these links he managed to get hold of one of the plants from the Andes and introduced it to his estates in Ireland.

The potato was not taken to readily. It was new and it was a member of the deadly nightshade family; both characteristics to make it unpopular with the Irish farmer. Within a century, however, its startling productivity and nutritional value had made it accepted. The popularity of the potato in Ireland reached almost unprecedented heights and it rapidly became the staple food of the population. It provides enough vitamins for most adults and is an excellent source of energy. This, together with the fact that it produces twice as much food to the acre as wheat and matures much more quickly in much poorer soil, made it ideal for Ireland.

The population boomed. It became practical to grow potatoes on the poor soils which had previously only supported sheep. Pigs were kept in sties and cattle in pens, and they were fed on potatoes to give meat and milk to families which might otherwise have only eaten potatoes. Cottages surrounded by a small farm became the dominant feature of the Irish landscape, even on the thin upland soils of the west. Large areas of land were drained or cleared, adding to the total of farmed land and removing the last vestiges of the natural landscape. A peculiar feature of Ireland was the practice of sub-letting. In this way a tenant farmer would re-let sections of his land to each of his sons as a marriage gift, and sub-let other parts to strangers in return for money. By 1841 this practice had been continued to such an extent that forty-five per cent of Irish farms were smaller than two hectares in extent and in Connaught only seven per cent were larger than six hectares.

In 1822 and 1836 partial failures of the potato crop had brought such hunger that it was clear to many that a great disaster was on the way. The only sure method was to enlarge the size of farms and decrease the dependence on potatoes. That in turn necessitated the eviction of large numbers of peasants. This made any landlord who attempted the feat incredibly unpopular and liable to victimisation. As a result the rural economy carried on with its dependence on potatoes and smaller holdings.

In 1845 potato blight struck Ireland and the entire potato crop failed. Starvation stalked the country for the next three years as the crop failed year after year. The government tried to help with relief works, but it achieved little. A million people died and many more emigrated before the solution was found in the form of new strains of potato. But the damage had been done and emigration continued. By the turn of the century the population of Ireland had dropped dramatically from more than eight million to less than four and a half.

The Great Famine had a decisive effect on the Irish landscape. The land once cleared to grow potatoes has been given over to more suitable crops. Sheep graze the mountains of the west which are kept bare of shrubs and trees to grow grass for the animals. The richer lowlands are devoted to dairy farming and arable crops. The present pattern of agriculture is the dominant force behind the shaping of Ireland's landscape. Without it the country would be a panorama of forests and bogland . Ireland still benefits from its warm, moist climate and the fertile soils with which it is endowed; it is still the green land that it has always been, though it is far removed from the land left by the retreating glaciers thousands of years ago.

Looking west from the clifftop above Great Stookan, County Antrim, with the low Mishowen Peninsula in the distance.

Wave and water erosion and periodic land slips have shaped the cliffs (above) east of the Giant's Causeway in County Antrim. Facing page: Benbane Head, east of the Giant's Causeway.

Above: Portrush in County Antrim, built on the narrow arm of Ramore Head. Facing page: sunshine on the fields of the north Antrim coast. Overleaf: (left) a peat-stained waterfall in Glenariff, and (right) farmland near Great Stookan, County Antrim.

28

Above: County Down farmland, seen from Scrabo Hill. Facing page: pastureland below the Mourne Mountains, County Down (these pages and overleaf). Overleaf left: Scrabo Tower, built in 1851 in memory of the third Marquis of Londonderry.

Above: roughened water on Spelga Reservoir, in the heart of the Mourne Mountains, and (facing page) the shore of Mahee Island on Strangford Lough, County Down.

Facing page: storm clouds over Lough Erne, and (above) low cloud and rain hide the Combe Mountains and obscure the outline of Lower Lough Erne, County Fermanagh. Overleaf: rivers in Gortin Glen Forest Park, County Tyrone.

Facing page: the Inishowen Peninsula, and (bottom) the beach at Castlerock, County Derry. Bottom right: Glenelly Valley, and (below) the Sperrin Mountains. Right: Mussenden Temple at Downhill, County Derry.

Left and bottom left: the Gap of Mamore, and (bottom) buildings in the Urris Hills, both on the Inishowen Peninsula, Donegal (these pages and overleaf). Below: Lough Swilly, and (facing page) the Atlantic from Greencastle. Overleaf: (right) farmland near the Grianan of Aileach (left).

Facing page: the rocky coast of Doagh Isle, and (above) the view across Lough Swilly from
the Grianan of Aileach, an ancient fort in County Donegal.

Above: St. Patrick's Purgatory on Station Island in Lough Derg, County Donegal (these pages and overleaf). Facing page: the lighthouse on Fanad Head. Overleaf: (left) Torneady Point, at the northern tip of Aran Island, and (right) Slieve League.

O' Rourke Castle (facing page) at Dromahair, County Leitrim, was once the
royal seat of Breffni. Top: Lough Ramor, County Cavan, and (above) Inner Lake,
in the Dartrey Forest, County Monaghan. Top right: Cooley Peninsula, and
(right) Dundalk Bay, County Louth.

Right and below left: waterfall at Glencar Lakes (below centre), Lough Key Forest Park, County Leitrim, and (bottom left) fishing boats in Kilkeel Harbour, County Down. Bottom right: a quiet golf course in the countryside of County Monaghan, and (facing page) donkeys in the green landscape of the Cooley Peninsula, County Louth. Overleaf: (left) the Georgian mansion of Headfort demesne at Kells (right), County Meath, the ancestral home of the Marquesses of Headfort.

Top: Benbulben in County Sligo (these pages). Above: Drumcliff Church, Yeats' burial place. Top right: Moneygold, and (right and facing page) Glencar Lough. Overleaf: (left) Hill of Slane, and (right) Slane Castle, County Meath.

Below: Downpatrick Head, and (right) Aasleagh Falls, near Leenane. Remaining pictures: farming in County Mayo (these pages and overleaf). Overleaf: (left) Ashford Castle, and (right) Croagh Patrick, a place of pilgrimage overlooking Clew Bay.

County Mayo's Killary Harbour (left and facing page) is considered one of the most beautiful inlets on the Irish coast. Below: the Twelve Bens in the distance beyond Clifden Bay, and (bottom and bottom left) Kingstown Bay, near Connemara.

Facing page: low, rocky Slyne Head, off the coast of County Galway (these pages), and (above) the sheer cliffs of Inishmore, one of the Aran Islands.

The countryside around Leenane (left), Ballynahinch (below), Roundstone (bottom left) and Ballynakill Bay (facing page) – through which the Dawros River makes its way – is typical of the green beauty of County Galway. Overleaf: (left) rushing, peat-coloured falls on the Owenriff River, and (right) dark water in Killary Harbour.

Above: Charleville demesne, Tullamore, and (facing page) the ruins of Clonmacnoise, a sixth-century monastery, both in County Offaly.

The building of Castletown House (right), County Kildare, was begun in 1722 by William Conolly, a speaker of the Irish Parliament. Below: 140-foot-high Conolly's Folly, built in 1740 by the Speaker's widow, Lady Louisa Conolly, to provide work after a hard winter. Bottom right: St. Patrick's College, Maynooth, was founded in 1795 on the site of an older, sixteenth-century college. Facing page: Carton House at Maynooth, County Kildare. Designed by Richard Cassels, the house dates from 1739. Overleaf: (left) rich farmland in hills near Athy, County Kildare, and (right) Poulaphouca Reservoir, fed by the waters of the River Liffey in County Wicklow.

Above and facing page: the Four Courts, the square spire of Christ Church Cathedral and Dublin Castle can be picked out in aerial views of Dublin (these pages and overleaf).
Overleaf: (left) O'Connell Bridge, and (right) the Halfpenny Bridge over the River Liffey.

82

These pages and overleaf: the architecture of Dublin. Right: Mansion House, (below) the General Post Office, (bottom) the National Gallery, (bottom right) Trinity College, (facing page) Leinster House. Overleaf: (left) Fitzwilliam Square, and (right) Merrion Square.

Facing page: the Grand Canal, Dublin (these pages). Top: *Eire*, by Jerome Connor, in Merrion Square Park (above). Top right: deer, and (right) fishing in Phoenix Park. Phoenix Park was established by the Duke of Ormonde.

Top: Glencree fields. Top right: the Great Sugar Loaf. Above: Glendalough Forest Park. Right: Glenmacnass. Facing page: a Wicklow stream. Overleaf: (left) Powerscourt House, and (right) Greystones.

Below: Dunbrody Abbey, built east of Waterford by Cistercian monks in about 1182. Below right: high seas off Hook Head Lighthouse, which guards the entrance to Waterford Harbour. East of Waterford, fishing boats crowd into the harbour of Kilmore Quay (right and facing page). Overleaf left: the J.F. Kennedy Memorial Park, an arboretum landscaped across the slopes of Slieve Caoilte in County Wexford. Further east, beautiful grounds surround the nineteenth-century Gothic Johnstown Castle (overleaf right).

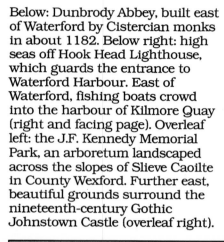

Above: the harbour at Wexford, with the River Slaney beyond, and (facing page) New Ross
in County Wexford, on the River Barrow.

Fields of stubble (facing page) in the Blackstairs Mountain region near Ballymurphy, County Carlow, and (left) on the plain of County Laois and County Kildare. Below left and below: views of the Laois countryside from the 200-foot-high Rock of Dunamase, site of an ancient fort. The later castle was reduced to its present ruins by the army of Oliver Cromwell in 1650. Overleaf: the agricultural land around Portlaoise, County Laois, seen from the Rock of Dunamase.

Above: landscape northwest of Kilkenny, County Kilkenny. Facing page: the River Suir, northwest of Waterford. Overleaf: (left) Inistioge on the River Nore, and (right) Graiguenamanagh on the River Barrow, County Kilkenny.

Facing page: Curraghmore House, County Waterford (these pages), seat of the Beresford family. Left: boats moored near Tramore, and (below) Bunmahon cliffs. Bottom and bottom left: the Comeragh Mountains.

Cashel (overleaf left), in the plain of Tipperary, is famous for Cashel Rock (above) on top of which stands its Cathedral, Cormack's Chapel, the Round Tower and the Cross of Cashel. At Cahir, County Tipperary (these pages and overleaf), stands the medieval Cahir Castle (facing page) of the Earl of Thomond and the Butlers, which was restored in 1840. Overleaf right: the dairy farming town of Tipperary on the River Ara, tracing its roots back to the twelfth century when King John built a castle there.

115

bottom right: the cliffs of Moore Bay near Kilkee. Remaining pictures: the cliffs of Moher, a five-mile stretch, rising some 700 feet above the Atlantic. right and bottom: O'Brien's Tower perched atop the cliffs.

117

The peace and solitude of a ruined fifteenth-century church (above) near ?aherconnell, in the Burren region of County Clare (these pages). Top: a view ?wards Spanish Point and the distant Atlantic.

Above: the River Lee running in two channels through Cork. Facing page: an aerial view of St. Colman's Cathedral (overleaf right), Cobh. Overleaf left: Father Mathew Memorial Church and Parliament Bridge over the south channel of the River Lee, Cork.

To kiss the famed Blarney Stone is said to bestow upon the individual the gift of eloquence – a quality for which the Irish are renowned. It is this stone, part of the fifteenth-century Blarney Castle (this page), which largely accounts for the fame of the town. Facing page and overleaf: the varied and beautiful countryside of County Cork, largest of the counties of Ireland.

Top: Knocknagallaun, in the Slieve Miskish Mountains of County Cork (these pages), (above) Adrigole Mountain, and (facing page) Adrigole Harbour on Bantry Bay. Top right: Glanworth bridge, and (right) Glenville bridge.

The Healy Pass road (facing page) snakes through the landscape of the Caha Mountains (this page) on the borders of counties Kerry and Cork. Overleaf: placid lakes and rushing streams epitomise the unspoilt beauty of the Iveragh Peninsula, County Kerry.

Facing page and below: Killarney, County Kerry (these pages and overleaf). Bottom centre: a signpost on the Killarney-Kenmare road. Remaining pictures: the Owenreagh River. Overleaf: (left) a river near Castlemaine, and (right) Connor Pass.

Facing page: Carrantuohill by Lough Acoose in Macgillicuddy's Reeks (above). Left and top left: Kenmare River. Top: the Slieve Miskish range. Overleaf: (left) Dingle Peninsula, and (right) Iveragh Peninsula.

When the sun breaks through the clouds, lighting the landscape of Doon Point (facing page), on the Dingle Peninsula, County Kerry, it is easy to understand the reason for the name 'Emerald Isle'. This northernmost of Kerry's peninsulas rejoices in some of the most picturesque of Ireland's landscapes, as at Smerwick Harbour, looking towards Three Sisters (left) and Kilmalkedar (bottom left), and (below) Inishtooskert Island from Dunquin. Overleaf: Slea Head on the Dingle Peninsula.